MEET THE MEGAFAUNA!

GABRIELLE BALKAN
ILLUSTRATED BY QUANG AND LIEN

WORKMAN PUBLISHING · NEW YORK

TO **AN OPEN BOOK FOUNDATION,**
FOR YOUR CHEERY AND STEADFAST
DEDICATION TO READERS AND
THEIR EDUCATORS. —GB

TO OUR DEAR NEPHEW,
D. PHÚC.
—PNQ AND HKL

For their excellent advice and consultation,

MEGA THANKS

to all who shouted thoughts to my animal-related
musings, including Anthony Friscia, PhD, associate
adjunct professor of integrative biology and physiology
at the University of California, Los Angeles, and
Michaela Warshaw, a fellow Barnard College graduate
with an added masters in museum anthropology from
Columbia University in New York City.

Copyright © 2023 by Workman Publishing Company, Inc.,
a subsidiary of Hachette Book Group, Inc.
Illustrations copyright © by Phung Nguyen Quang and Huynh Kim Lien

Library of Congress Cataloging-in-Publication Data is available.

ISBN 978-1-5235-0860-0

Design by Sara Corbett
Cover illustration by Phung Nguyen Quang and Huynh Kim Lien

Workman books are available at special discounts when purchased in bulk for
premiums and sales promotions as well as for fundraising or educational use.
Special editions or book excerpts can also be created to specification. For details,
please contact special.markets@hbgusa.com.

Workman Publishing Co., Inc., a subsidiary of Hachette Book Group, Inc.
1290 Avenue of the Americas
New York, NY 10104

WORKMAN is a registered trademark
of Workman Publishing Co., Inc., a subsidiary of Hachette Book Group, Inc.

Printed in China
First printing July 2023
10 9 8 7 6 5 4 3 2 1

CONTENTS

WHAT ARE MEGAFAUNA?

Long before you or anyone you know was born, giant beasts walked the earth. A few of these giants are still alive today. One hundred ten million years ago, there were crocodiles so long they would have needed a bed the size of a fire engine to nap in. Twenty million years ago, there were rhinoceroses six times heavier than any alive today. As recently as six hundred years ago, there were birds so tall they would have towered over the top of some swing sets. Today, the blue whale is longer than two school buses and so gigantic it needs thousands of pounds of food every single day. These magnificent beings are all megafauna.

Megafauna are any animals that have grown to supersized proportions. Some scientists describe megafauna as animals that are significantly larger than their closest modern relative, as you'll see with many of the animals in this book. The abundance of food, habitat, and oxygen available in the Cretaceous, Paleogene, Neogene, and early Quaternary periods helped animals grow to great sizes. We do not have these same abundances today.

Scientists learn about the past by studying fossils. It's rare to find a complete skeleton of an extinct animal. Sometimes, part of the skeleton has been eaten or dragged away by a scavenger; other times, sections have been carried away by flood, buried by rubble, crushed during construction work, or even excavated by an amateur archaeologist.

In the best-case scenario, a team of paleontologists would discover several entire skeletons from both male and female animals at different stages of their lives. More likely, a team uncovers a handful of bones from an adult female, another handful of different bones from an adolescent male, and maybe a single bone from an infant. With just a few bones, scientists then estimate the size of the entire body by comparing it to what we have observed in animals alive today.

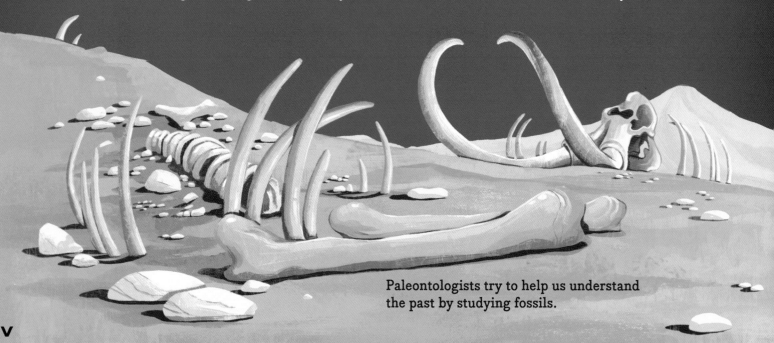

Paleontologists try to help us understand the past by studying fossils.

There are a few things to keep in mind while you consider the estimated measurements in this book:

Height measurements run from foot to shoulder. The head is not included.

Length measurements run from snout to rump. The tail (if there is one) is usually not included. When an animal's tail *is* included in their complete length, this book includes the symbol * in the animal's information box (see Supercroc, page 1).

Just as with people, the size of each animal varies, in part based on what food is available to them and the size of their biological parents. Some animals have extreme size differences depending on whether they are male or female. This book lists the estimated size that goes along with the largest of the species and notes whether it is a female, male, or—if the fossil record is not clear—unknown.

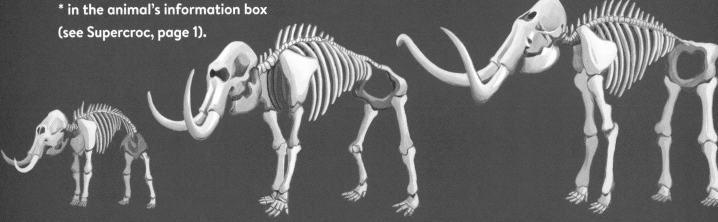

Just like humans, the size of animals in the same species varies.

WHERE AND WHEN DID THEY LIVE?

For millions of years during and following the Cretaceous period, these massive animals thrived in nearly every part of the world. They lived in warm climates close to the equator and frigid areas near the North and South Poles. In different parts of the world, different types of megafauna flourished. Most megafauna became extinct around 10,000 years ago. Some are still alive today, though many of those are in danger of going extinct.

Geologists, scientists who study the liquids, gases, and solids that make up the earth, measure periods of time using a geologic timescale. It divides the history of the earth into smaller units of time based on major events in the history of life. We name these units to make it easier to talk about and understand what has happened in our earth's history. Turn the page for more information about measuring geologic time. Then continue on to explore the world of megafauna.

MEASUREMENTS

THE
BIG
BANG

Eon: An eon is the largest span of time. Geologists have named four eons. Megafauna first came into existence during our current eon, the Phanerozoic eon, which began about 542 million years ago.

Era: The next largest measurement of geologic time is an era. An era is defined by the fossil life formed during that time period. There are three eras in our current eon, the Phanerozoic.

Period: Within each era, we measure periods. There are twelve in the Phanerozoic eon.

Epoch: Even though an epoch is one of the smaller measurements of geologic time, each one still spans millions of years. There are thirty-four epochs in all; they are only measured in our current eon.

We live in the Holocene epoch, Quaternary period, Cenozoic era, and Phanerozoic eon.

THE CRETACEOUS PERIOD

It was the last period of the Mesozoic era and spanned from 145 through 66 million years ago. During this period, nonbird dinosaurs went extinct; the big supercontinent, Pangea, continued breaking apart; and oceans formed along with the continents we know today. The supercroc and the giant turtle lived during this period.

Pangea was a supercontinent that was made of almost all of the landmasses on Earth.

THE PALEOGENE PERIOD

Small mammals lived among giant mammals, finding ways to survive—and thrive.

It was the first period of the Cenozoic era and spanned from 66 through 23 million years ago. During this period, mammals evolved from simple, small creatures into diverse, large ones. The giant snake and giant rhinoceros lived during this period.

OF GEOLOGIC TIME

PROTEROZOIC EON

PHANEROZOIC EON
CENOZOIC ERA

PALEOZOIC ERA | MESOZOIC ERA

CRETACEOUS PERIOD
PALEOGENE PERIOD

NEOGENE PERIOD
QUATERNARY PERIOD

THE NEOGENE PERIOD

It was the second period of the Cenozoic era and spanned from 23 through 2.6 million years ago. During this period, continents crashed into each other, mountains formed, and land bridges were created. These geological changes allowed animals to migrate to different parts of the world, changing the makeup of prey, predator, and plant life. The giant pig, giant shark, giant teratorn, giant ground sloth, and terror bird lived during this period.

Mountains formed when continents crashed into each other.

THE QUATERNARY PERIOD

It is the third period of the Cenozoic era and began 2.6 million years ago. It continues to the present day. During this period, glaciers advancing from the poles and then retreating changed the shape of land. Our current epoch, the Holocene, began around 11,650 years ago, when humans started making a significant impact on Earth. The South Island giant moa, saber-toothed cat, giant ape, giant armadillo, giant wombat, giant monitor lizard, giant deer, and woolly mammoth lived during this period. The African savanna elephant, blue whale, and Masai giraffe first appeared and are still living in this period.

Many animals began to go extinct as humans came on the scene and hunted them for food and clothing.

SUPERCROC

Last seen on Earth around 110 million years ago

The supercroc—*Sarcosuchus imperator*—is one of the fiercest predators of the mid-Cretaceous period. Including her tail, this particular beast is 40 feet (12 meters) long, weighs 17,500 pounds (7,938 kilograms), and rules the lush forests and rivers where she lives. Most of the supercroc's weight is wiry muscle, packed into a coat of armor made of bone and scales. This collection of interlocking scutes—or thick, bony plates— covers every inch of the reptile's back. It is unlikely that any creature has teeth or claws substantial enough to puncture her armor. When she hunts, she uses her 20-foot- (6-meter-) long tail as a spring to thrust herself from the water and capture her prey. Her 5-foot- (1.5-meter-) long jaw is like a steel trap that no animal can escape once locked in its grip. As a fully grown adult, she can overpower any animal.

SCIENTIFIC NAME *Sarcosuchus imperator*
MEANING "flesh crocodile emperor"
TIME PERIOD Cretaceous period
YEARS ACTIVE ca. 2 million years, from ca. 112 through 110 million years ago
PLACES LIVED what is now Africa and South America
CLASS reptile
LENGTH (SEX UNKNOWN) 40 ft* (12 m*)
WEIGHT (SEX UNKNOWN) 17,500 lb (7,938 kg)
MODERN RELATIVE saltwater crocodile; population stable, least concern

The only known difference between modern crocodilians and the supercroc is size. Both have growth spurts through adulthood and then continue to grow more slowly for as long as they are alive. Including their tails, the length of the saltwater crocodile is about 10 feet (3 meters) for females and 23 feet (7 meters) for males. Cretaceous crocs were about twice as long and eight times as heavy as the largest croc alive today.

The supercroc is a carnivore. She will eat anything she can catch, usually fish and turtles, but if the opportunity presents itself, she'll feast on a medium-sized, plant-eating dinosaur like a hadrosaur. The acid in her stomach helps her digest bones, hooves, shells, and any other body part that is unfortunate enough to have made its way in. She can go up to two years without eating, and her body can store what it doesn't immediately need. But she will never turn down a meal.

The supercroc was last seen around 110 million years ago. We don't know why this magnificent reptile vanished. We formulate our ideas of what they were like by observing the more than twenty species of crocodilians alive today. They hatch by the dozens from eggs, spend their days basking in small groups in the sun, lie still waiting for a meal, and fear virtually nothing.

GIANT TURTLE

Last seen on Earth 65 million years ago

Join us on a swim. You won't have to dive too deep. The giant turtle spends his days skimming the surface of the water looking for food. As an omnivore, he'll dine on a mix of jellyfish, squid, and the ever-present seaweed. *Archelon ischyros* is the world's largest sea turtle. Including his tail, he is 15 feet (4.6 meters) long and weighs 4,500 pounds (2,200 kilograms).

His powerful flippers slice through the water with the efficiency of an oar. A hooked beak cracks open the hard shells of marine animals. But his most marvelous feature is his shell. At first glance, it looks like one supersized piece of solid bone. But a solid shell would be so heavy it would drag him to the bottom of the ocean. Instead, the thin carapace—or shell—is made of a framework of widely spaced ribs covered with thick leathery skin.

The only time this reptile has been out of the sea was the day he was born. Every year, mother turtles head to the beach to bury dozens of eggs deep into dry sand. Then they return to the ocean. For two to three months, the eggs are protected by the sand. When they're ready to hatch, each turtle uses its beak to break out of its shell. Then they head for the safety of the water. For infants, this relatively short journey across the beach is full of peril. Many are snatched up by flying reptiles called pterosaurs. As an adult, this turtle is too big for many predators. Mosasaurs are his main worry. Luckily, experience has taught him how to evade and outswim these threats. So far.

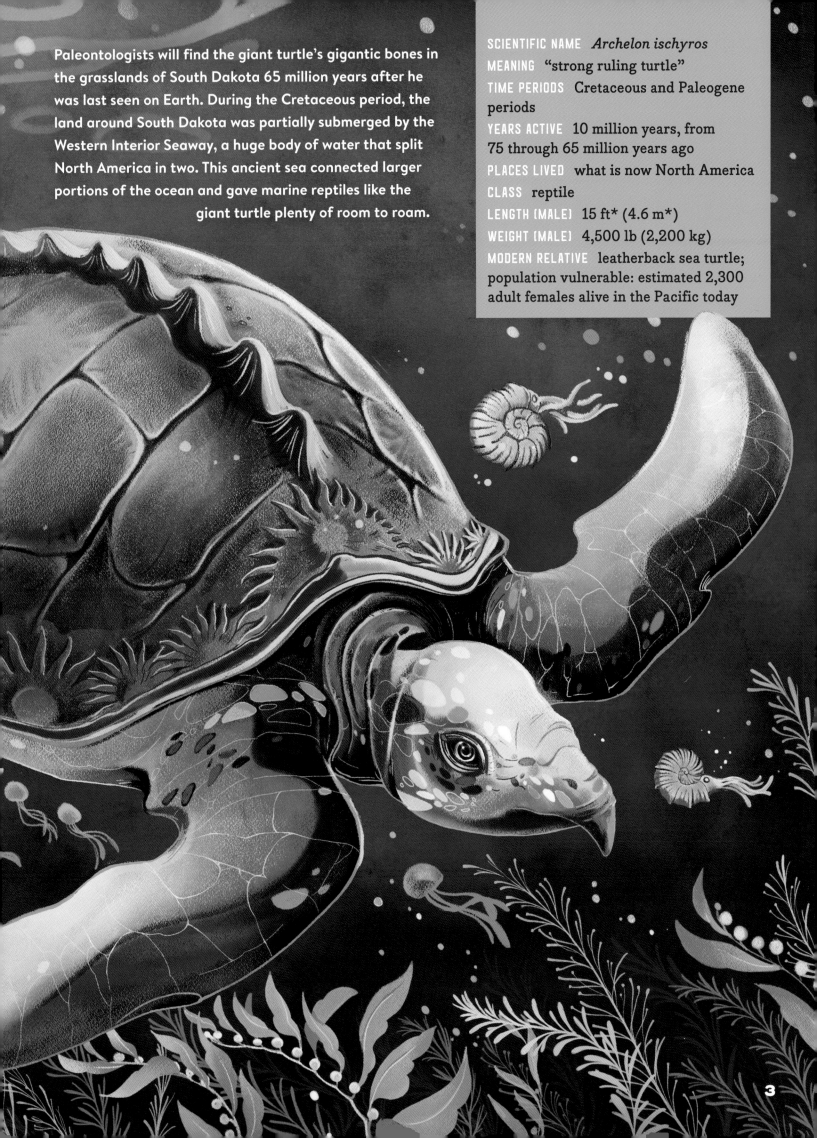

Paleontologists will find the giant turtle's gigantic bones in the grasslands of South Dakota 65 million years after he was last seen on Earth. During the Cretaceous period, the land around South Dakota was partially submerged by the Western Interior Seaway, a huge body of water that split North America in two. This ancient sea connected larger portions of the ocean and gave marine reptiles like the giant turtle plenty of room to roam.

SCIENTIFIC NAME *Archelon ischyros*
MEANING "strong ruling turtle"
TIME PERIODS Cretaceous and Paleogene periods
YEARS ACTIVE 10 million years, from 75 through 65 million years ago
PLACES LIVED what is now North America
CLASS reptile
LENGTH (MALE) 15 ft* (4.6 m*)
WEIGHT (MALE) 4,500 lb (2,200 kg)
MODERN RELATIVE leatherback sea turtle; population vulnerable: estimated 2,300 adult females alive in the Pacific today

GIANT SNAKE

Last seen on Earth 48 million years ago

SCIENTIFIC NAME *Titanoboa cerrejonensis*
MEANING "titanic boa from Cerrejón"
TIME PERIOD Paleogene period
YEARS ACTIVE 10 million years, from ca. 58 through ca. 48 million years ago
PLACES LIVED what is now South America
CLASS reptile
LENGTH (SEX UNKNOWN) 50 ft* (15.2 m*)
WEIGHT (SEX UNKNOWN) 2,500 lb (1,134 kg)
MODERN RELATIVE green anaconda; population unknown, least concern

If you're quiet and step carefully, you might catch sight of the giant snake before she catches sight of you. You can listen, but it won't do you any good; the giant snake doesn't make any sound—until it's too late. *Titanoboa cerrejonensis* is 50 feet (15.2 meters) long and weighs 2,500 pounds (1,134 kilograms), making her the largest snake the world has ever seen. She is so enormous that each of the vertebrae in her back is the size of a grapefruit. She sticks close to the equator in warm waters and climates like those found in South America today. She eats 5-foot- (1.5-meter-) wide turtles, 20-foot- (6-meter-) long crocodiles, and fish. She'll swallow each whole, after wrapping her oversized body around them and squeezing them to a slow, unmerciful death.

To find her prey, this majestic reptile lurks deep underwater. With her eyes trained upward, she watches until a suitable meal presents itself. She can hold her breath for forty-five minutes. She never blinks; snakes don't have eyelids. Instead, a transparent scale covers each eye, protecting the eye from floating debris and the claws of fighting prey. She spends most of her time in the water. It's the easiest landscape for a body as heavy as hers.

Once she's captured her prey, it's time to eat. Her jawbones loosen, letting her mouth full of sharp, closely packed teeth open a gaping 180 degrees. This is how she can swallow creatures the size of a croc. Her muscles contract to pull her meal through her long throat and into her stomach.

Just like snakes alive today, the giant snake needed warm temperatures to grow. The extreme warmth of the Paleogene period led to this carnivore's extreme size. When the earth's temperature became cooler, the giant snake could not grow as large and eventually died out. The largest snakes today can be found in the same warm climates of South America. Boas like the 550-pound (249-kilogram) and 29-foot- (8.8-meter-) long green anaconda have many of the same traits.

GIANT RHINOCEROS

Last seen on Earth 23 million years ago

GIANT PIG

Last seen on Earth 19 million years ago

I t looks to be a perfect day. There's a bright sun and a slight breeze, and it's not too hot yet. But an ugly drama is about to begin. Two *Daeodon shoshonensis*—giant piglike creatures—have barged in on a bear dog and now feast on the camel she took down. These 12-foot- (3.7-meter-) long and 2,000-pound (907-kilogram) pigs aren't very clever. They don't plan complicated hunting strategies. Instead, they use their tremendous bodies to bully their way into food scraps.

The giant pig has a varied collection of teeth: sharp front teeth for tearing flesh from bone, hard canines to dig for roots, and flat molars for grinding plants, berries, and nuts. An excellent sense of smell helps them sniff out the scent of a dead animal. They bite at each other's faces and when they are done fighting, they run away on strong legs.

Paleontologists have only found a few giant rhinoceros bones. At first, they thought the shape of these bones meant the ancient beasts looked like modern-day wide-mouthed rhinoceroses. But they now suspect that *Paraceratherium* did not have a horn and looked more like a tapir, a modern piglike mammal that has a short, prehensile nose trunk and can weigh up to 660 pounds (299 kilograms). Either way, paleontologists estimate that a *Paraceratherium* could weigh as much as eight modern rhinos or fifty tapirs! Paleontologists are not sure why this awesome animal disappeared but think it might have had to do with the arrival of the elephant. The elephant's useful prehensile trunk allowed it to eat a wider variety of plants, and it might have eaten so much that the giant rhino ran out of food.

SCIENTIFIC NAME *Paraceratherium transouralicum*
MEANING "near the hornless beast"
TIME PERIODS Paleogene and Neogene periods
YEARS ACTIVE ca. 11 million years, from ca. 34 through ca. 23 million years ago
PLACES LIVED what is now Asia and Europe
CLASS mammal
LENGTH (SEX UNKNOWN) 26 ft (7.9 m)
HEIGHT (SEX UNKNOWN) 16 ft (4.9 m)
WEIGHT (SEX UNKNOWN) 33,000 lb (14,969 kg)
MODERN RELATIVE wide-mouthed rhinoceros; population decreasing, near threatened: estimated 10,080 mature individuals

The evening air is windless and without rain, but thankfully, the temperature has dropped. The cool night is a welcome relief from the roasting sun of the day and inspires friendly nickers from young giant rhinoceroses. Every evening, this herd of *Paraceratherium transouralicum* plods miles and miles, slowly moving through the grassland looking for food. As herbivores, they power their enormous bodies with nothing but vegetation. They eat upward of 500–600 pounds (227–272 kilograms) a day and rely on the soft leaves at the tops of tall trees, which no other animal can reach. Their prehensile lips can grasp like fingers and pluck leaves from the trees with a funny sucking sound.

Their appetites satisfied for now, they've paused their march and joined another small herd near a muddy watering hole. These giant rhinos range in age from preteens to elder matriarchs, the female herd leaders. The biggest among them weigh 33,000 pounds (14,969 kilograms) and, from snout to rump, reach 26 feet (7.9 meters) long. They are the largest land mammals of all time.

It's amazing that animals this size play, but they do. It's a good night for games. There isn't a crocodile, one of their biggest predators, in sight. A few carnivores scamper around, but the number of giant rhinos in the herd keeps these doglike carnivores in check. Even so, watchful mothers observe from a close distance. If a croc appears and attempts to threaten one of their babies, the giant mothers will charge, aiming to frighten the reptile with a heavy stomp from one of their massive feet. Young rhinos are easily overpowered, so they survive adolescence by keeping close to the safety of the herd.

As adults, these beasts are too big to have even a single predator, but they don't lead a peaceful life. The males wage constant battles for territory, food, and mates. Whoever comes out victorious in this clash wins the meal. The other will have to look for another dead animal to scavenge.

Despite having the nickname "Terminator Pig," *Daeodon* was not a pig at all. Paleontologists named it a pig based on early discoveries of the animal's molars. Later, when they learned more about its jaws and hooves, they speculated that it was more closely related to a hippopotamus. Either way, the head of the giant pig could grow to a shocking 3 feet (1 meter) long, which is larger than the heads of modern pigs or hippos. We don't know exactly how much these omnivores ate. Based on modern hippos, the largest *Daeodon* might have eaten as little as 30 pounds (14 kilograms) of food a day, which is low for other animals of this size but common for the hippo. Scientists speculate that a combination of factors contributed to its demise, the most significant being new carnivores that moved into the giant pig's territory and started competing for food.

SCIENTIFIC NAME *Daeodon shoshonensis*
MEANING "dreadful teeth"
TIME PERIODS Paleogene and Neogene periods
YEARS ACTIVE 10 million years, from 29 through 19 million years ago
PLACES LIVED what is now North America
CLASS mammal
LENGTH (SEX UNKNOWN) 12 ft (3.7 m)
HEIGHT (SEX UNKNOWN) 6.5 ft (2 m)
WEIGHT (SEX UNKNOWN) 2,000 lb (907 kg)
MODERN RELATIVE common hippopotamus; population stable but vulnerable: estimated 130,000 individuals

GIANT SHARK

Last seen on Earth 3.6 million years ago

With a mighty spray, the world's largest fish bursts into the air. Her gigantic mouth is wide open, exposing an awe-inspiring array of 276 teeth. The giant shark twists her body, flips her tail, and plunges back into the water.

This is *Carcharocles megalodon*, otherwise known as the "meg." She is 100,000 pounds (45,359 kilograms) of firm muscle and lightweight cartilage. She is so colossal that the distance between her front fins—24 feet (7 meters)—is greater than the length of the largest great white shark alive today. She stays close to the surface of the ocean, where there is a lot to eat. Her teeth are each 7 inches (17.8 centimeters) long, and some weigh more than 1 pound (0.5 kilograms)—perfect for catching a dolphin or other sea animal. She aims to eat 2,500 pounds (1,134 kilograms) of meat a day.

Her size and strength make her an apex predator, meaning that as a fully grown adult, there is no animal that dares to hunt her. Her glorious body is protected by dermal scales that are rough to the touch and overlap like the shingles on a roof. These scales exist in sharks alive today, too. In fact, some 2,700 years ago, before the invention of sandpaper, ancient Greeks used shark skin to smooth surfaces. In the ocean, these interlocking scales push water along the shark's body, allowing the beast to move through the ocean quickly.

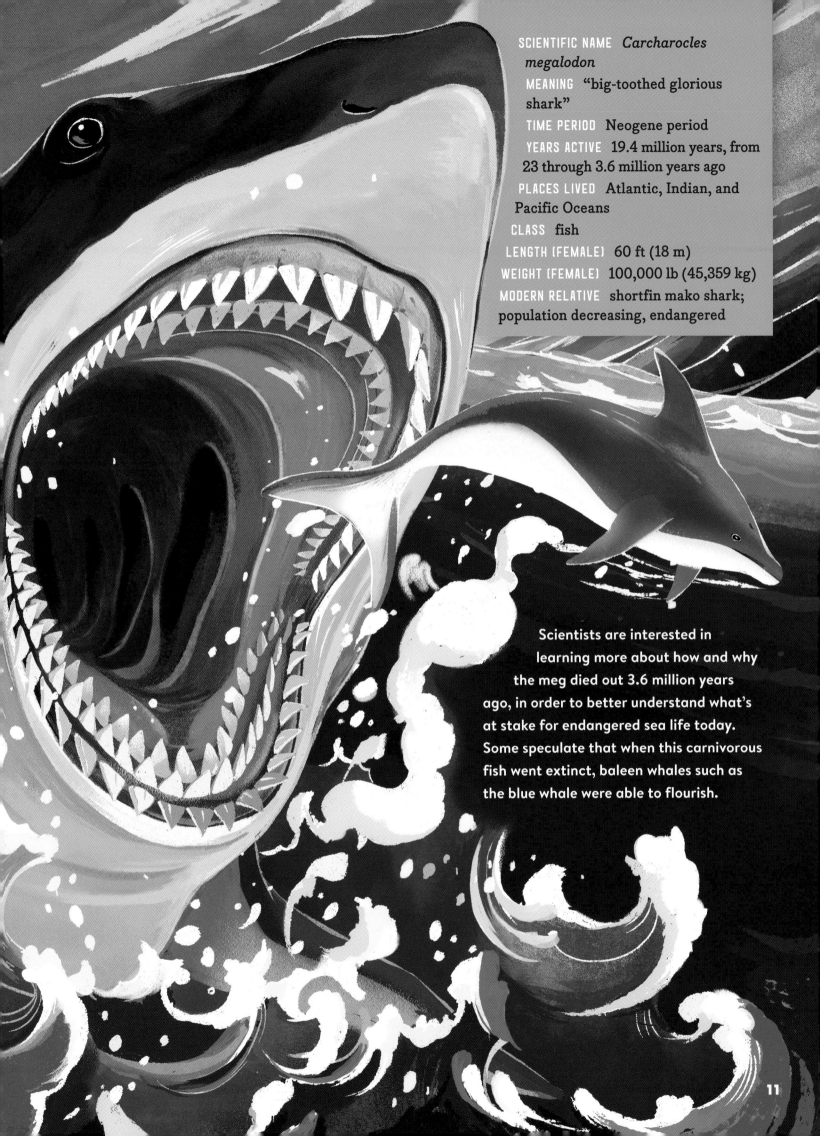

SCIENTIFIC NAME *Carcharocles megalodon*

MEANING "big-toothed glorious shark"

TIME PERIOD Neogene period

YEARS ACTIVE 19.4 million years, from 23 through 3.6 million years ago

PLACES LIVED Atlantic, Indian, and Pacific Oceans

CLASS fish

LENGTH (FEMALE) 60 ft (18 m)

WEIGHT (FEMALE) 100,000 lb (45,359 kg)

MODERN RELATIVE shortfin mako shark; population decreasing, endangered

Scientists are interested in learning more about how and why the meg died out 3.6 million years ago, in order to better understand what's at stake for endangered sea life today. Some speculate that when this carnivorous fish went extinct, baleen whales such as the blue whale were able to flourish.

GIANT TERATORN

Last seen on Earth 6 million years ago

Five miles above the earth, a stately beast patrols the sky. His immense wings stretch 10 feet (3 meters) from either side of his body, giving him a 23-foot (7-meter) wingspan. At 154 pounds (70 kilograms), he weighs nearly five times as much as his closest living relative, the 33-pound (15-kilogram) Andean condor. This is *Argentavis magnificens*, a giant teratorn, one of the largest birds the world has ever known.

SCIENTIFIC NAME *Argentavis magnificens*
MEANING "magnificent Argentine bird"
TIME PERIOD Neogene period
YEARS ACTIVE 2 million years, from
8 through 6 million years ago
PLACES LIVED what is now South America
CLASS bird
HEIGHT (SEX UNKNOWN) 6.5 ft (2 m)
WINGSPAN (SEX UNKNOWN) 23 ft (7 m)
WEIGHT (SEX UNKNOWN) 154 lb (70 kg)
MODERN RELATIVE Andean condor;
population decreasing, vulnerable:
estimated 6,700 mature individuals

Though the hot, dry day is perfect for flying, this is no leisurely outing. This jumbo-sized carnivore is stalking prey. He has already flown 100 miles (161 kilometers) today in search of food. He eats about 20 pounds (9 kilograms) of meat a day. He trains his keen eye downward, looking for an animal that's exactly the right size. Too small, and it won't be worth landing for. Too big, and he won't be able to knock it out with one blow and then swallow it whole.

Giant teratorns spend most of their time soaring. They are master gliders. Their long, heavy wings require a lot of effort to flap but are perfectly engineered to catch air thermals, columns of rising air. To catch one, the teratorn looks for puffy, cottonlike cumulus clouds. Once the giant teratorn identifies a thermal, he circles around it, and is able to rise through the air and soar to the next thermal. This is how he can glide mile after mile without a single flap, conserving valuable energy.

Members of the superb teratorn family soared the skies for a total of two million years, a rather short span of time in the history of our planet. No teratorns survived the Neogene period, perhaps because of how slowly they were thought to reproduce.

GIANT GROUND SLOTH

Last seen on Earth 11,700 years ago

criiiitch. That's the sound of two sets of claws ripping through the rough bark of a tree. These switchblade-sharp nails belong to *Megatherium americanum*, a giant ground sloth. Including his tail, he is 20 feet (6 meters) long, weighs 8,818 pounds (4,000 kilograms), and is so powerful he can uproot a tree.

At the moment, this fantastic herbivore is peeling bark to eat. Not many creatures can digest vegetation this tough, but the giant ground sloth has a specialized digestive system that lets him make good use of the bark and the hardy, moisture-filled leaves at the top of the tree. He uses his sturdy tail like a third leg, helping him keep his balance as he reaches up 12 feet (3.7 meters) high. Then he can grasp the leaves with his prehensile tongue, which is able to grip and hold objects on its own.

SCIENTIFIC NAME *Megatherium americanum*
MEANING "great beast from America"
TIME PERIOD Neogene period
YEARS ACTIVE ca. 5.29 million years, from ca. 5.3 million years through ca. 11,700 years ago
PLACES LIVED what is now South America
CLASS mammal
LENGTH (SEX UNKNOWN) 20 ft* (6.1 m*)
WEIGHT (SEX UNKNOWN) 8,818 lb (4,000 kg)
MODERN RELATIVE brown-throated three-toed sloth; population unknown, least concern

The giant ground sloth brings his front paws to the ground with a thud. He throws his vast body against the tree, giving his side a good scratch. This mammal is covered in coarse, shaggy fur. It keeps him warm and protects him during scuffles with other animals. He is unique among the various giant sloth species in that he does not have small, round bone plates, called osteoderms, underneath his skin. In his relatives, these tiny bones act like chain mail, making the beast nearly indestructible—and one of nature's oddities. The armadillo is the only other mammal to have these bones.

His most awe-inspiring feature is his set of claws. Each of his claws is about 7 inches (18 centimeters) long and as sharp as a dagger. He uses them primarily for scratching off bark and digging shelter. His claws are too long for him to walk flat-footed, so he walks on the outside of his back feet. The result is a slow waddling motion. Giant ground sloths are not built for speed.

Unfortunately for the giant ground sloth, his slow speed makes him a target for the prehistoric humans in the area. Our distant ancestors stalked giant sloths, stepping in their exact footprints to follow them across the grasslands. They hunted in groups, perhaps in twos, with one to distract and confuse the sloth while the other would sneak up from behind to deliver a fatal blow. The enormous mammal would provide meat and clothing. Plus, if the hunters could find his burrow, they could use it for shelter.

TERROR BIRD

Last seen on Earth 1.8 million years ago

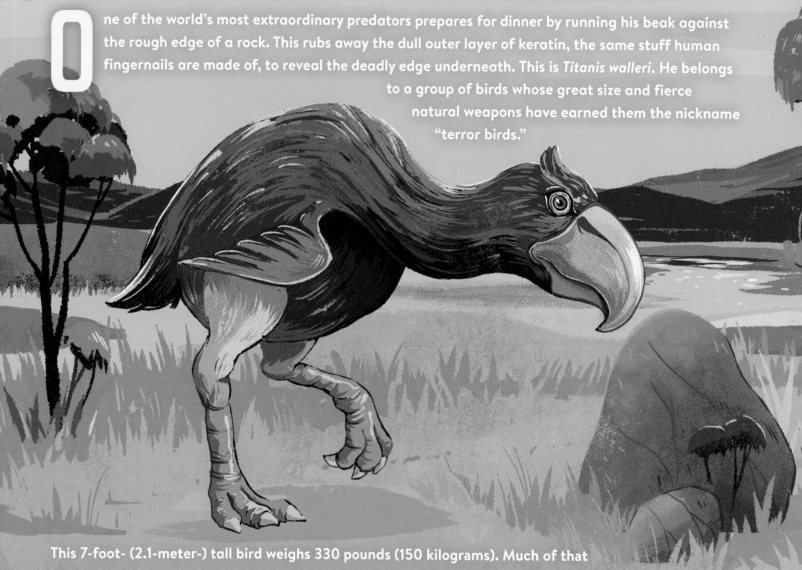

One of the world's most extraordinary predators prepares for dinner by running his beak against the rough edge of a rock. This rubs away the dull outer layer of keratin, the same stuff human fingernails are made of, to reveal the deadly edge underneath. This is *Titanis walleri*. He belongs to a group of birds whose great size and fierce natural weapons have earned them the nickname "terror birds."

This 7-foot- (2.1-meter-) tall bird weighs 330 pounds (150 kilograms). Much of that weight is solid muscle. None of the twenty or so species of terror bird can fly; they weigh too much, and the muscles around their smallish wings are not strong enough to lift them off the ground. They are built to run, though, and they can run fast, around 40 miles (64 kilometers) per hour. Once he reaches his prey, the carnivorous bird has a number of strategies he can deploy. He might kick at it with feet powerful enough to break bones. Or, he can make a severe swipe with one of the claws on his extra-long toes. Once the animal has fallen, he keeps it in place with a hooked front talon. Then he grasps it in his beak so he can lift it and smash it to the ground. Finally, he'll use his beak like a pickax to peck at the animal, ripping off big pieces of flesh to swallow whole.

There is still much to learn about these mighty creatures. Up until recently, scientists had miscalculated their size, thinking these hulking birds were even larger, and their diet more robust. You might find illustrations that suggest that these animals were large enough to eat a horse, but scientists no longer think this is true. Their modern-day relative, the red-legged seriema, is much smaller, weighing a mere 6 pounds (2.7 kilograms) and standing just 3 feet (1 meter) tall. Even so, she shares her ancestor's scrappy hunting ability. With the discovery of more fossils, we might learn that the extinct terror bird had even more in common with today's seriema.

SCIENTIFIC NAME   *Titanis walleri*

MEANING   *Titanis* refers to the giant ancient Greek gods, the Titans. *Walleri* is a nod to an archaeologist.

TIME PERIODS   Neogene and Quaternary periods

YEARS ACTIVE   3.2 million years, from 5 through 1.8 million years ago

PLACES LIVED   what is now North America and South America

CLASS   bird

HEIGHT (SEX UNKNOWN)   7 ft (2.1 m)

WEIGHT (SEX UNKNOWN)   330 lb (150 kg)

MODERN RELATIVE   red-legged seriema; population stable, least concern

SOUTH ISLAND GIANT MOA

Last seen on Earth 600 years ago

A clutch of downy chicks peers through the bright green vegetation. With a little coaxing from their monumental, 11.8-foot- (3.6-meter-) tall mothers, these chicks tumble out of their nest. It's time to eat! They're still young but already able to forage for grub on their own. These herbivores are *Dinornis robustus*, better known as South Island giant moas.

SABER-TOOTHED CAT

Last seen on Earth 13,000 years ago

SCIENTIFIC NAME *Smilodon fatalis*

MEANING "deadly knife tooth"

TIME PERIOD Quaternary period

YEARS ACTIVE 2,487,000 years, from 2.5 million through 13,000 years ago

PLACES LIVED what is now North America and South America

CLASS mammal

LENGTH (SEX UNKNOWN) 5.8 ft (1.8 m)

HEIGHT 3 ft (1 meter)

WEIGHT (SEX UNKNOWN) 617 lb (280 kg)

MODERN RELATIVE African lion; population decreasing, vulnerable: estimated 39,000 mature individuals

Moas had a very recent and abrupt extinction. Scientists are still learning exactly what led to their complete wipeout, but one thing they know for certain: In addition to the Haast's eagle, many animals liked the taste of moa, including humans, such as the Māori people. These indigenous Polynesians arrived in New Zealand around one thousand years ago. While the skilled hunters quickly learned strategies for capturing the grown moas, their dogs easily devoured the tiny chicks. And the rats that stowed away in the canoes of the Māori went after the eggs.

We'll never see another moa, but we can observe their distant relative today, the much smaller tinamou, which lives in Central and South America. Like the moa, female tinamous are larger than the males of their species. Recent 3D-scanning technology has allowed scientists to see tiny details in the tinamou's throat. These scans reveal that living tinamous breathe, communicate, and eat in similar manners as their extinct relatives. The next mystery to unravel is how a flightless bird such as the moa managed to have descendants half a world away from New Zealand.

The moa's long, swanlike windpipe produces deep, loud calls used to communicate danger or interest in mating, depending on the situation. Today, it's a warning. One has caught a glimpse of a Haast's eagle, the moa's main predator and the largest eagle in the world. The eagle is big and strong enough that it could easily strike down a 500-pound (227-kilogram) moa. Moas are flightless—they can't flee to the skies. Instead, they scramble back into the dense undergrowth, counting on the muted stripes of their feathers to camouflage their hefty bodies.

In addition to gobbling down berries, seeds, and leaves, these grand birds also eat rocks. Moas have no teeth, so they swallow rocks to perform the grinding function of molars. From inside the moa's stomach, these gastroliths, or gizzard stones, break the food into smaller, easier-to-digest bits. With each meal, the gastrolith grinds itself smoother. In time, the stone will no longer be rough enough to break down the moa's food, so the moa will cough it up and find another.

SCIENTIFIC NAME *Dinornis robustus*
MEANING "strong terrible bird"
TIME PERIOD Quaternary period
YEARS ACTIVE ca. 2,579,400 years, from ca. 2.58 million through ca. 600 years ago
PLACES LIVED what is now New Zealand
CLASS bird
HEIGHT (FEMALE) 11.8 ft (3.6 m)
WEIGHT (FEMALE) 500 lb (227 kg)
MODERN RELATIVE tinamou; population stable, least concern

GIANT APE

Last seen on Earth 100,000 years ago

A pair of bright eyes peers out from behind a mass of wide green leaves. They belong to a very still, very patient five-year-old *Gigantopithecus blacki*. Though this giant ape is still young, he will one day grow to be nearly 10 feet (3 meters) tall and weigh up to 661 pounds (300 kilograms), making him the largest primate the world has ever known. As an adult, his enormous size and strength will keep him safe from every predator in his range. For the next three years, however, the young herbivore still requires the attentive gaze of his mother.

While the little ones play, their mother grabs at a piece of bamboo to chew, exposing her oversized teeth. Her back molars are nearly an inch wide and an inch long. She'll use them to eat leaves, lots of fruit, and other plants found on the forest floor. She grabs and pulls at a long branch. She's fashioning a sort of umbrella to use once the rain starts. She uses her toes to hold the branch in place while her hands twist it into the right shape. The giant ape is able to use her toes to pick up and manipulate items. Like all apes, she is highly intelligent and able to craft all sorts of tools to make her life easier.

Sabertooths hunt in packs, and two female members of the pride, or family group, are out doing the heavy lifting. The alpha female plots a path that allows her to creep along the treeline for as long as she can. When she gets close enough, she will leap, hoping to surprise her meal before it can bolt. She uses her powerful forelimbs to take down the prey while the other sabertooth bites into its neck.

After the hunt, the alpha returns to the spot where she left her cubs. The other mighty cat stays behind and continues eating as the rest of the members of the pride join in. The cubs are play-fighting in a bush a few yards from where their mother left them. As soon as they spot her, they bound over, hungry for a meal of their own. At just two months old, these cubs have not yet started eating meat and rely on their mother's milk for nourishment.

Even though the now-extinct sabertooth was an apex predator, meaning no animals hunted it for food, they did encounter plenty of danger. After all, there was not just *one* 617-pound (280-kilogram) beast, but many of them, each looking for something to eat and someplace to live. Based in part on the number of bones found together, scientists suspect that saber-toothed cats lived in a pride, similar to one of their closest modern-day relatives, the African lion. And like African lions today, each pride would have hunted, bonded, mated, and taken care of the sick in its own territory.

The decline of the saber-toothed cat was probably caused by their great size and the decreasing size of other mammals in the area. The big cat was used to hunting large mammals, such as the 2,299-pound (1,043-kilogram) black rhinoceroses, and as those disappeared, the cat was unable to adjust to hunting smaller animals and starved.

I t's just about dusk, and the day's blindingly bright sun is about to set. From her observation spot behind a mass of pale yellow grass, an athletic predator sees something she likes: a herd of camel-like, long-necked herbivores. The predator is *Smilodon fatalis*, a saber-toothed cat. She is 500 pounds (227 kilograms) of lean muscle. Her strength is impressive, but it's her razor-sharp teeth that her prey need to worry about. Each of her front canine teeth is 8 inches (20 centimeters) long—too long to be covered by her lip. It's been a few days since this carnivore's last meal, and her stomach rumbles. It's time to hunt. But first, she must hide her young.

It is likely that when climate changes turned the ape's forested home into grassy savannas, the jumbo-sized creature could not find enough food to support its immense size. We don't know exactly how much these dignified herbivores ate. Their diet depended on the time of year and where they lived. They may have eaten around 110 pounds (50 kilograms) of food a day.

Paleoanthropologists, scientists who study the fossils of primates (including humans), and paleontologists, who study the fossils of all animals and plants, are especially interested in studying great apes like *Gigantopithecus* because of their close genetic relationship with humans. The Hominidae family includes this giant ape and the great apes that followed, including bonobos, chimpanzees, gorillas, orangutans, and human beings. In addition to physical similarities like opposable thumbs, all members share complex intellectual traits. The most significant is the ability to recognize themselves in mirrors and be self-aware.

SCIENTIFIC NAME *Gigantopithecus blacki*
MEANING "giant ape discovered by Black"
TIME PERIOD Quaternary period
YEARS ACTIVE 1,900,000 years, from 2 million to 100,000 years ago
PLACES LIVED what is now Asia
CLASS mammal
HEIGHT [SEX UNKNOWN] 10 ft (3 m)
WEIGHT [SEX UNKNOWN] 661 lb (300 kg)
MODERN RELATIVE Sumatran orangutan; population decreasing, critically endangered: estimated 13,846 individuals

GIANT ARMADILLO

Last seen on Earth 10,000 years ago

Fwooosh! CRASH! Two colossal mammals fight over territory. One has strayed too far from his usual turf. The other is irritated. Though he's hungry and would rather focus on grazing on grass, this herbivore can't let an interloper pass through unchallenged. These are two glyptodonts, otherwise known as giant armadillos. Including their tail, the largest among them is 13 feet (4 meters) long and weighs 5,220 pounds (2,368 kilograms).

Each magnificent armadillo is protected by what looks like an enormous domed shell but is actually a set of some 2,000 tightly fitted bone plates, known as scutes. In addition to their armor, the mammals are dotted with fur. Tufts of hair poke out and act as sensors, giving the giant armadillo information about its environment. It is a necessary sense for a creature whose eyesight is not very sharp.

This particular species, *Doedicurus clavicaudatus*, is famous for its tail, which is highly flexible and ends with ironlike spikes. The tough bones on top of its head do an excellent job protecting its face from the sharp teeth of predators but make it hard to see. It's nearly impossible for the giant armadillo to aim its blows.

Climate change and human hunting led to the giant armadillo's extinction at the end of the last ice age, seven thousand years ago. There are, however, twenty varieties of armadillo alive today. The largest, the tatou, can weigh up to 180 pounds (81.6 kilograms), while the smallest, the pink fairy armadillo, weighs less than a pound. For each species, evolution held on to the armadillo's most spectacular trait: its protective scutes. Armadillos are the only living mammals with this type of bone covering. Still, many of the armadillo species alive today are at risk of becoming extinct like their massive ancestor. Their natural habitats and food sources have been taken over by humans, who use the land to grow crops and construct buildings.

SCIENTIFIC NAME *Doedicurus clavicaudatus*
MEANING "pestle tail"
TIME PERIOD Quaternary period
YEARS ACTIVE 1,490,000 years, from 1.5 million to 10,000 years ago
PLACES LIVED what is now South America
CLASS mammal
LENGTH (SEX UNKNOWN) 13 ft* (4 m*)
HEIGHT (SEX UNKNOWN) 5 ft (1.5 m)
WEIGHT (SEX UNKNOWN) 5,220 lb (2,368 kg)
MODERN RELATIVE pink fairy armadillo; population unknown, research needed

AFRICAN SAVANNA ELEPHANT

Still living today in parts of Africa, including
the Masai Mara National Reserve, Kenya

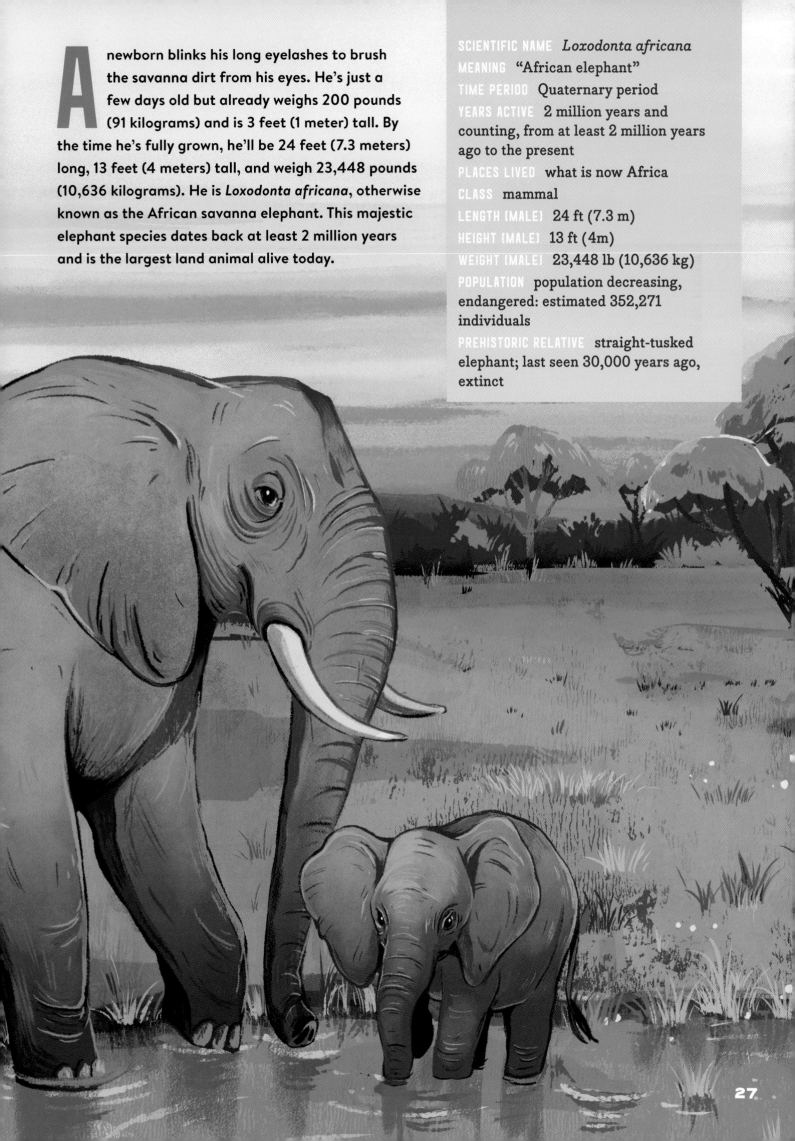

A newborn blinks his long eyelashes to brush the savanna dirt from his eyes. He's just a few days old but already weighs 200 pounds (91 kilograms) and is 3 feet (1 meter) tall. By the time he's fully grown, he'll be 24 feet (7.3 meters) long, 13 feet (4 meters) tall, and weigh 23,448 pounds (10,636 kilograms). He is *Loxodonta africana*, otherwise known as the African savanna elephant. This majestic elephant species dates back at least 2 million years and is the largest land animal alive today.

SCIENTIFIC NAME *Loxodonta africana*

MEANING "African elephant"

TIME PERIOD Quaternary period

YEARS ACTIVE 2 million years and counting, from at least 2 million years ago to the present

PLACES LIVED what is now Africa

CLASS mammal

LENGTH (MALE) 24 ft (7.3 m)

HEIGHT (MALE) 13 ft (4m)

WEIGHT (MALE) 23,448 lb (10,636 kg)

POPULATION population decreasing, endangered: estimated 352,271 individuals

PREHISTORIC RELATIVE straight-tusked elephant; last seen 30,000 years ago, extinct

Even though it's early yet, the stately herd is already on the move. The focus, as always, is food. They'll each eat upward of 200 pounds (91 kilograms) of grasses, fruits, and leaves and drink 50 gallons (189 liters) of water in just one day. They move slowly, only 4 miles (6.4 kilometers) per hour. These massive herbivores don't need speed to protect themselves—their size keeps lions and other predators away.

There are three species of elephant alive today, and *Loxodonta africana* is the largest. Scientists believe all species of modern elephant are related to the extinct mammoth, mastodon, and straight-tusked elephant. The straight-tusked elephant was about the same height as the African savanna elephant but twice as heavy. Even without predators, the African savanna elephant is in danger of becoming extinct. Humans have slowly taken away its natural habitat, destroying trees and plants and building factories in those places. And, even though it is illegal to do so, some humans hunt elephants to steal their ivory tusks.

From this point on, the elder female elephants will help the clumsy newborn mammal with everything. His eyesight will take a long time to sharpen, and he'll need their help to nurse, lumber in and out of watering holes, and stay clear of lions. The elder females will even teach him how to use his sophisticated prehensile trunk. It is strong enough to uproot a tree, flexible enough to pick up a single leaf, and gentle enough to stroke a loved one. He'll learn to use his trunk to pull in 2 gallons (7.6 liters) of water and then tip it into his throat for a big gulp. When he swims, he can send his trunk above the water to use it as a snorkel.

GIANT WOMBAT

Last seen on Earth 25,000 years ago

The gentle huffing of a giant wombat can be heard across the outback. This oversized wombat carries her joey in her snug pouch as she uses her athletic front legs and sharp claws to dig up delicious plants to eat. She is a *Diprotodon optatum*, the world's largest marsupial. She is 12 feet (3.7 meters) long, weighs 6,000 pounds (2,700 kilograms), and is covered with stiff, shaggy fur. As an herbivore, she eats far more than 100 pounds (45 kilograms) of shrubs and flowering plants a day. She sticks close to the lake for easy access to the water.

For at least 20,000 years, these beautiful lumbering beasts coexisted with the Aboriginal people indigenous to Australia. Based on the marks on some giant wombat fossils, some anthropologists speculate that indigenous Australians may have used spears to hunt the exceptional animal. The wombat's substantial body would have provided ample food and fur. This is not what led to the animal's demise, however. During the Pleistocene epoch, much of Australia experienced extreme droughts, leaving little water or plants for the giant wombat to eat.

Based on observing marsupials today, scientists believe that the giant wombats did not live in large herds and were somewhat solitary creatures.

SCIENTIFIC NAME *Diprotodon optatum*
MEANING "two forward teeth"
TIME PERIOD Quaternary period
YEARS ACTIVE 24.98 million years, from 25 million through 25,000 years ago
PLACES LIVED what is now Australia
CLASS mammal
LENGTH (MALE) 12 ft (3.7 m)
HEIGHT (MALE) 6 ft (1.8 m)
WEIGHT (MALE) 6,000 lb (2,700 kg)
MODERN RELATIVE coarse-haired wombat; population stable, least concern

Unlike other marsupials, the giant wombat has a pouch that opens to the rear. This protects the joey's face from flying dirt as his mother digs. Baby wombats are born blind, deaf, hairless, and at a size too small to survive outside of the pouch. But after six months, they will be covered in thick fur and will soon leave the pouch.

GIANT MONITOR LIZARD

Last seen on Earth
50,000 years ago

SCIENTIFIC NAME *Megalania prisca*
MEANING "ancient great roamer"
TIME PERIOD Quaternary period
YEARS ACTIVE ca. 1,450,000 years, from
ca. 1.5 million through ca. 50,000
years ago
PLACES LIVED what is now Australia
CLASS reptile
LENGTH (SEX UNKNOWN) 11 ft (3.4 m)
WEIGHT (SEX UNKNOWN) 1,370 lb (621 kg)
MODERN RELATIVE Komodo dragon;
population stable, endangered: estimated
1,383 mature individuals

The sun blazes through the middle of the day. There's not a drop of moisture to be felt or a cloud to be seen. The world's largest monitor lizard has retreated from the heat to the relative cool of a shallow burrow. This is *Megalania prisca*. She is 11 feet (3.4 meters) long and weighs 1,370 pounds (621 kilograms). Her enormous body is covered in tough scales that act like chain mail, protecting her from anyone who would dare attack. Few will; she mostly needs protection from members of her own reptilian species, who may try to steal her meal.

Her long, thick tongue flicks in and out. This is how she smells: Each time her tongue flicks out, it collects scent particles from the air and directs them toward the roof of her mouth. Smell is this carnivore's most valuable sense—it points her toward a meal and away from a threat.

When the day cools, she'll creep across the desert at a steady, stealthy pace. She's an opportunistic eater and will happily eat other reptiles, birds, and even large mammals such as the giant kangaroo and the giant wombat. When she needs to eat, she'll knock down her prey with a mighty swipe from her tail and bite off a chunk of flesh with sharp, serrated teeth.

Based on scattered and incomplete fossilized bones, scientists estimate that this extraordinary lizard went extinct around 50,000 years ago. Because so few fossilized bones have been found, scientists aren't quite sure how big this giant lizard actually was. Early estimates, based on mostly jaw bones and a few arm bones, put the beast at 20 feet (6 meters) long. But most agree now that the giant lizard was probably about half that length. Some scientists think *Megalania prisca* released venomous saliva to make her prey weak and easier to overcome. However, other scientific evidence says this is not true.

She dives deep, heading 200 feet (61 meters) below the surface, looking for food. Eating is an all-day activity for an animal as huge as this. This carnivore will need to consume 8,000 pounds (3,629 kilograms) of krill, small shrimplike sea creatures, in just one day. To feed, she expands her giant mouth to take in 3,500 gallons (13,249 liters) of salt water and krill in one gulp. Then she pushes the water back out through the three hundred 3-foot- (1-meter-) long flexible baleen plates that she has instead of teeth. These plates act as a sieve, letting the water flow out and leaving the blue whale with a belly full of protein.

BLUE WHALE

Still living today in all regions of
the ocean except the Arctic

The blue whale travels through every ocean in the world except for the chilly Arctic. Come winter, this marvelous mammal will migrate roughly 4,000 miles (6,437 kilometers) from the cooler waters near the North Pole toward the warmer waters near the equator. She makes this trip to breed and raise a baby whale, called a calf. She'll carry her calf in her womb for about twelve months, a surprisingly short amount of time for an animal this massive. The calf enters the world at a whopping 25 feet (7.6 meters) long and 6,000 pounds (2,722 kilograms). For the first year of his life, he'll feast on 50 gallons (189 liters) of milk a day and gain 8 pounds (3.6 kilograms) an hour for a total of 200 pounds (91 kilograms) a day. By the time he's an adult, he'll weigh 330,700 pounds (150,003 kilograms).

MASAI GIRAFFE

Still living today in parts of Africa, including Tanzania

Seemingly without warning, a herd of giraffes breaks into a gallop, kicking up clumps of grass and making an astonishing clamor with each step of their mighty 12-inch- (30.5-centimeter-) diameter hooves. These are *Giraffa camelopardalis tippelskirchi*, better known as Masai giraffes. They race across the grasslands, moving away from an unseen danger. With their 6-foot- (1.8-meter-) long legs and 6-foot- (1.8-meter-) long necks, they have an incredible sight line for approaching predators. The males are 19 feet (5.8 meters) tall and top the scales at 4,250 pounds (1,928 kilograms).

These beautiful beasts are covered in a pattern of rusty oranges and browns that is as unique as a fingerprint—no two animals have the same markings. The pattern helps regulate their body temperature. Under each brown patch is a cluster of blood vessels that collect the heat and then push it out from their body.

Eventually, the grand herd slows. Who knows what spooked them. The group returns to their usual cluster, forming an expansive patchwork of browns, creams, and oranges. Standing in a tight-knit group makes it tricky for any hungry hyenas to see where one giant animal ends and the other begins.

The blue whale as we know it has explored the oceans for 1.5 million years. For much of that time, they had substantial numbers. However, the species is now in danger of going extinct. Blue whales face some threats from orca whales, their only natural predator, but much of their decline is caused by human activities that endanger their habitat with microplastics and noise pollution.

Thousands of miles from shore, the world's largest animal explodes through the ocean's surface with a tremendous splash. *Balaenoptera musculus*, better known as the blue whale, is the largest animal to *ever* live on Earth. The mammal is 100 feet (30.5 meters) long and so heavy that her weight is nearly impossible to comprehend. The female clocks in at more than 400,000 pounds (181,437 kilograms), heavier than the space shuttle *Endeavour*, thirty times as heavy as an African savanna elephant, and heavier than the males of her species. She is too big to exist on land. It is only the buoyancy of the water combined with her blubber that keeps the weight of her tremendous body from crushing her skeleton. Her tongue alone weighs around 6,000 pounds (2,722 kilograms), and her heart clocks in at around 1,500 pounds (680 kilograms).

This gentle beast has been underwater for the past hour. She exhales the breath she's been holding, and it looks like a geyser exploding, sending a spray of water nearly 30 feet (9.1 meters) into the sky. Then she takes a deep breath before a sturdy flap covers her two blowholes to keep water out. Her massive lungs store enough oxygen for her to hold her breath for another sixty minutes.

SCIENTIFIC NAME *Balaenoptera musculus*
MEANING "winged whale with muscle"
TIME PERIOD Quaternary period
YEARS ACTIVE 1.5 million years and counting, from 1.5 million years ago to the present
PLACES LIVED all regions of the ocean except the Arctic
CLASS mammal
LENGTH (FEMALE) 110 ft* (33.5 m*)
HEIGHT (FEMALE) 13 ft (4 m)
WEIGHT (FEMALE) 400,000 lb (181,437 kg)
POPULATION increasing, endangered: estimated 15,000 mature individuals
PREHISTORIC RELATIVE *Pakicetus*; last seen ca. 42 million years ago, extinct

SCIENTIFIC NAME *Giraffa camelopardalis tippelskirchi*

MEANING "spotted camel discovered by Tippelskirch"

TIME PERIOD Quaternary period

YEARS ACTIVE 1 million years and counting, from 1 million years ago to the present

PLACES LIVED what is now Africa

CLASS mammal

LENGTH (MALE) 8.5 ft (2.6 m)

HEIGHT (MALE) 19 ft (5.8 m)

WEIGHT (MALE) 4,250 lb (1,928 kg)

POPULATION population decreasing, endangered: estimated 35,000 mature individuals

PREHISTORIC RELATIVE Shiva's beast; last seen 8,000 years ago, extinct

One by one, the giraffes take up eating again, as peaceful as ever. One uses her highly flexible, prehensile, 18-inch (45.7-centimeter), blue-black tongue to grasp the leaves of an acacia tree, the giraffe's favorite meal. The leaves are covered in thorns, but the giraffe's tongue is protected by small, thick bumps called papillae. Giraffes get much of their water from the leaves of the acacia tree. The rest of the day, a total of up to twenty hours in all, will be spent eating. They'll eat up to 165 pounds (75 kilograms) of leaves a day.

The Masai giraffe made its first appearance one million years ago and is one of the few megafauna species still alive today. For thousands of years, adult giraffes' great size protected them from most predators. Though young giraffes are small enough to be taken down by predators such as lions, giraffe mothers are fiercely protective, and most predators know that they could suffer a skull-crushing kick if they hassle a calf. However, with the arrival of humans came weapons that outpowered the giraffe's mightiest kick. Some humans hunt giraffes for meat, but a more significant danger comes from poachers, who kill these beasts to make jewelry from their tail-hair and bone carvings to sell to tourists. Because of this, there are fewer than 120,000 giraffes left in Africa and only 45,000 of the Masai variety.

GIANT DEER

Last seen on Earth 11,000 years ago

A phenomenal cloud of dust fogs the air, kicked up by the hooves of a deer larger than any alive today. The giant deer bolts this way and that, making sure the width of his antlers is easy for his competition, another huge male, to see. He is *Megaloceros giganteus*, known as the giant deer. He is nearly 10 feet (3 meters) long and weighs 1,500 pounds (680 kilograms). His antlers are the most impressive thing about him: They weigh 88.2 pounds (40 kilograms) and stretch 12 feet (3.7 meters) from tip to tip.

SCIENTIFIC NAME *Megaloceros giganteus*
MEANING "big-horned giant"
TIME PERIOD Quaternary period
YEARS ACTIVE 389,000 years, from 400,000 through 11,000 years ago
PLACES LIVED what is now Asia and Europe
CLASS mammal
LENGTH (MALE) 9.8 ft (3 m)
HEIGHT (MALE) 7 ft (2.1 m)
WEIGHT (MALE) 1,500 lb (680 kg)
MODERN RELATIVE fallow deer; population unknown, least concern

It happens like clockwork every year: mating season. The bucks have now fully regrown their antlers. After every mating season, male deer produce less testosterone, a change that makes their antlers fall off. After the antlers are shed, they are then regrown the following spring. Each time a buck regrows its antlers, they grow back tougher, larger, and, usually, with an additional point. The size of his antlers will help this mammal attract a doe. A buck that is healthy enough to grow such monumental ornaments and strong enough to carry them will probably have the necessary genes to help the doe have a healthy fawn.

A couple of does watch the battle, their noses working overtime. They have an excellent sense of smell and can smell a predator even before seeing one. Their sense of smell is their primary defense against animals like the dire wolf, a large canine that is among their biggest threats. Should they smell one, these does will quickly dash off. Speed is another of the giant deer's defenses against predators, and even fawns can walk within hours of being born.

The giant deer species thrived for about 389,000 years until it died out 11,000 years ago. One theory of their extinction proposes that the herbivore's selective diet of calcium-rich willow made it a challenge to find enough to eat once climate change affected the plants that grew in its habitat.

WOOLLY MAMMOTH

Last seen on Earth 4,000 years ago

t's hard to hear much other than the deafening roar of the wind. Dense flurries of snow make it difficult to see. A thick layer of ice covers every square inch of the ground. The temperature has already fallen well below freezing, and it will get colder come nightfall. Not many animals would find these elements welcoming, but thanks to generations of clever evolutionary adaptations, the herd of *Mammuthus primigenius* is quite comfortable. These are woolly mammoths, megafauna royalty of the ice age. These 16-foot- (4.9-meter-) long, 16,000-pound (7,257-kilogram) beasts have relatively small, furry ears and short tails that reduce heat loss and prevent frostbite. Their thick, shaggy hair grows 3 feet (1 meter) long, helping them survive frigid temperatures as they trudge across the flat steppes of northern Russia. Three layers of hair and a chubby layer of fat have insulated these gigantic mammals so well, they hardly notice the snow. However, if the slashing wind gets to be too much for even these cold-loving mammoths, they can huddle close in a herd of around twenty warm bodies.

A pair of mammoths uses the sharp points at the ends of their graceful white tusks to clear a path through the ice so they can enjoy the grasses and plants that lie underneath. By the end of the day, these herbivores will each have eaten around 500 pounds (227 kilograms) of vegetation.

Scientists know more about the remarkable woolly mammoth than any other prehistoric animal. This is in part because, in some isolated parts of the world, humans spent at least 2,000 years living among mammoths before these megafauna became extinct just 4,000 years ago. Humans hunted the mammoth and made good use of its entire body. They used its meat for food and its shaggy coat for warmth, and built huts out of mammoth bones. The mammoth was so vital to early humans that our ancestors painted countless pictures of them on cave walls. This, along with a good collection of skeleton findings, has given us an excellent idea of what these glorious creatures looked like.

SCIENTIFIC NAME *Mammuthus primigenius*
MEANING "first earth animal"
TIME PERIOD Quaternary period
YEARS ACTIVE ca. 3.9 million years, from 3,896,000 through 4,000 years ago
PLACES LIVED what is now Asia, Europe, and North America
CLASS mammal
LENGTH (MALE) 16 ft (4.9 m)
HEIGHT (MALE) 11 ft (3.4 m)
WEIGHT (MALE) 16,000 lb (7,257 kg)
MODERN RELATIVE Asian elephant; population decreasing, endangered: estimated 40,000 individuals

WHERE DID THEY GO?

There are four main factors that can lead to any animal's extinction: drastic changes in the environment, the scarcity of food, an increase in animal competition, and the loss of habitat. No single event is enough to cause a complete wipeout, but when multiple events happen around the same time, the outcome can be dire. Here's a bit more information about how these factors can play out:

TEMPERATURE SHIFTS

A significant shift in Earth's temperature allowed some megafauna to grow very large; and then, when Earth went through another sudden temperature change, their bodies could not adapt quickly enough. In addition, temperature shifts changed the type and abundance of plant life available. Some megafauna could not find enough of the food they needed to thrive.

SHIFTING LAND MASSES

As land masses changed shape, animals began to travel into new territories. That meant there were more animals competing for food, both plants and prey. Those that were able to adapt and change their diet survived. Those that had a specialized diet and couldn't adapt went extinct.

EARLY HUMANS

The arrival of humans was a significant factor in the extinction of some megafauna. Just as some humans do today, early humans hunted animals for food and used their skins and furs for clothing.

LONGER REPRODUCTION

Large animals tend to have fewer offspring that require longer reproduction periods. Some megafauna took nearly two years to develop in their mother's womb. Combined with food shortages from competing animals and death from human hunters, animals with long reproduction times could not reproduce quickly enough to keep their species from dying out.

PROTECTING TODAY'S MEGAFAUNA

We can work together to protect megafauna that are alive today. Environmental activists strive to pass laws that protect animal habitats so they can find enough food to eat and have safe places to raise their young without threat of human hunting or building. Some activists promote vegetarian and vegan diets and non-animal-based clothing choices. One great way to help protect megafauna is to learn about them and share what you have learned with others. In this way, you increase interest in protecting the animals' habitats.

Here are some of the many modern megafauna that need our help:

THE EASTERN GORILLA lives in the Virunga
Mountains, a chain of volcanoes along the borders of the Democratic Republic of the Congo, Rwanda, and Uganda. Males are much larger than females and typically weigh around 353 pounds (160 kilograms) and stand 6 feet (1.8 meters) tall. They are the world's largest living primates. Habitat destruction, illegal hunting (called poaching), disease, and slow reproductive rates have placed these mammals on the list of critically endangered species. There are an estimated 2,600 adults left in the wild.

THE KOMODO DRAGON is native to Indonesia. Males can weigh up to 330 pounds (150 kilograms) and reach a length of more than 10 feet (3 meters). They are the heaviest lizards on the planet. Illegal hunting and habitat clearance are among the threats placing this reptile on the list of species moving toward extinction. There are an estimated 1,383 adults left in the wild.

THE SIBERIAN TIGER

is found primarily in Russia, with smaller populations in China and North Korea. Males can weigh up to 660 pounds (299 kilograms) and reach 10.75 feet (3.3 meters) long. They are the world's largest cats. Forest destruction and poaching have placed this mammal on the list of threatened species. There are an estimated 400 adults left in the wild.

THE SHORTFIN MAKO SHARK

lives in tropical oceans around the world. Females can weigh up to 1,200 pounds (544 kilograms) and reach lengths of 12.5 feet (3.8 meters). They are the world's fastest sharks and among the world's fastest fish. Overfishing by humans is the main reason these fish have been added to the list of endangered species. The number of adults left in the wild is unknown.

THE SOUTHERN CASSOWARY lives in

Australia, New Guinea, and nearby islands. Females can weigh up to 167 pounds (75.7 kilograms) and reach 5.6 feet (1.7 meters) tall. They are the world's second heaviest birds after the 320-pound (145-kilogram), 9-foot- (2.7-meter-) tall ostrich. Habitat loss, car collisions, and human hunting are some of the factors that placed this bird on the endangered species list in 1999. But communities worked hard to give this species a comeback. As of 2018, it was no longer endangered.

MEGAFAUNA WORDS

Some of these words are most often used when talking about the study of fossils; others you will know from reading about animals in general.

apex predator (*noun*): An animal at the top of the food chain, who, as an adult, has no natural predators. For instance, no animal preyed on the adult saber-toothed cat (page 20), making it an extinct apex predator.

carnivore (*noun*): An animal that eats animal flesh, either by hunting or scavenging, rather than plants. The terror bird (page 16) was a carnivore.

SEE ALSO: herbivore, omnivore.

class (*noun*): A classification into which animals are grouped based on the way they look, behave, and reproduce. The megafauna in this book belong to one of these four classes: bird, fish, mammal, or reptile.

SEE ALSO: species.

Cretaceous period (*noun*): In geology, the period of time spanning from 145 through 66 million years ago. It was the last period of the Mesozoic era. During this period, nonbird dinosaurs went extinct, big land masses continued to shift, and oceans formed.

SEE ALSO: Neogene period, Paleogene period, Quaternary period, Geologic Time (page vi).

eon (*noun*): In geology, the largest span of time. Geologists have named four eons. The first eon began 4.6 billion years ago and lasted for 600 million years.

SEE ALSO: epoch, era, period, Geologic Time (page vi).

epoch (*noun*): In geology, the fourth-largest period of time. There are thirty-four epochs in the Phanerozoic era. We live in the Holocene epoch. An epoch, which usually includes several million years, is shorter than a period and is subdivided into smaller periods of time called ages.

SEE ALSO: eon, era, period, Geologic Time (page vi).

era (*noun*): In geology, the second-largest period of time, measured by the fossil life formed during that time period. There are four eras in the Phanerozoic eon. We live in the Cenozoic era. *Periods* and *epochs* are smaller groups of time within an era.

SEE ALSO: eon, epoch, period, Geologic Time (page vi).

genetic *(adjective):* The genetic relationship between animals describes how different features are passed along from parent to offspring. All living organisms have genes, made up of DNA.

herbivore *(noun):* An animal that eats plants, rather than flesh. The giant rhinoceros (page 6) was an herbivore.

SEE ALSO: carnivore, omnivore.

evolution *(noun):* In biology, a gradual change to a species over generations, often as a way to adapt to a series of conditions in the animal's environment.

megafauna *(noun):* Megafauna refers to any animal that has grown to oversized proportions. Most megafauna have no natural predators capable of killing them as adults.

extant *(adjective):* Referring to an animal species that is still in existence today. The blue whale is one of the few extant megafauna.

SEE ALSO: extinct.

Neogene period *(noun):* In geology, the period of time spanning 23 million years ago through 2.6 million years ago. It was the second period of the Cenozoic era. During this period, continents crashed into each other, mountains formed, and land bridges were created.

SEE ALSO: Cretaceous period, Paleogene period, Quaternary period, Geologic Time (page vi).

extinct *(adjective):* Referring to an animal species that is no longer in existence. The giant ape went extinct 100,000 years ago.

SEE ALSO: extant, What Are Megafauna? (page iv).

fossil *(noun):* The remains of any living organism, such as a plant or animal, that have been preserved in the earth's crust.

SEE ALSO: paleoanthropologist, paleontologist.

omnivore *(noun):* An animal that eats both plants and animal flesh. The giant pig (page 8) was an omnivore.

SEE ALSO: carnivore, herbivore.

opposable (*adjective*): In anatomy, capable of touching to the other digits on the same hand or foot. Humans have opposable thumbs; saber-toothed cats do not.

SEE ALSO: primate.

paleoanthropologist (*noun*): A scientist who studies the fossils of primates, including great apes and humans.

SEE ALSO: fossil, paleontologist.

Paleogene period (*noun*): In geology, the period of time spanning from 66 million years ago through 23 million years ago. It was the first period of the Cenozoic era. During this period, mammals evolved from simple, small creatures into diverse, large ones.

SEE ALSO: Cretaceous period, Neogene period, Quaternary period, Geologic Time (page vi).

paleontologist (*noun*): A scientist who studies the fossils of animals and plants.

SEE ALSO: fossil, paleoanthropologist.

period (*noun*): In geology, the third-largest period of time, longer than an epoch and shorter than an era. There are twelve periods in the Phanerozoic eon, and we live in the Quaternary period.

SEE ALSO: eon, epoch, era, Geologic Time (page vi).

predator (*noun*): An animal that hunts other animals for food. The terror bird was a predator that hunted small mammals as prey.

SEE ALSO: prey.

prehensile (*adjective*): Able to wrap around something and grasp it. Prehensile body parts in animals can include tails, as in some monkeys and seahorses; trunks, as in elephants and tapirs; and tongues, as in giraffes and some sloths.

SEE ALSO: opposable

prehistoric (*adjective*): Before the time of written records.

prey (*noun*): An animal that is hunted and killed for food. Prey animals often have eyes on the sides of their heads so they can have a better field of vision.

SEE ALSO: predator.

primate *(noun)*: In zoology, a member of a group of mammals that includes monkeys, apes, and humans. Key features include forward-facing eyes, hands with opposable digits, and feet that are similar to their hands. Primates usually dwell in trees.

SEE ALSO: opposable.

Quaternary period *(noun)*: In geology, the period of time spanning from 2.6 million years ago to present day. It is the third period of the Cenozoic era. During this period, glaciers advancing from the poles and then retreating changed the shape of land.

SEE ALSO: Cretaceous period, Neogene period, Paleogene period, Geologic Time (page vi).

species *(noun)*: In biology, a group of animals that have the same characteristics and together are capable of creating children that can also reproduce. For instance, humans (*Homo sapiens*) are one species, and chimpanzees (*Pan troglodytes*) are another. Both of these species fall under the scientific classification family of great apes (Hominidae). The name of the species is always written in italics.

SEE ALSO: class.

FURTHER CONNECTIONS

I f you enjoy learning about megafauna and what life was like millions of years ago, you might enjoy connecting with these organizations and resources. Remember to ask a grown-up's permission before using the internet and to always use safe internet practices.

AT THE LIBRARY

Apex Predators by Steve Jenkins, Houghton Mifflin Harcourt Books for Young Readers, 2020

DK Eyewitness Books: Prehistoric Life by William Lindsay, DK Publishing, 2012

Explorer: Mammals! by Nick Forshaw and William Exley, What on Earth Books, 2019

Extinct: An Illustrated Exploration of Animals That Have Disappeared by Lucas Riera, illustrated by Jack Tite, Phaidon Press, 2019

The Magic School Bus in the Time of the Dinosaurs by Joanna Cole, illustrated by Bruce Degen, Scholastic, 1995

Prehistoric World (Usborne World History) by Fiona Chandler, Sam Taplin, and Jane Bingham, Usborne, 2000

Visions of Lost Worlds: The Paleoart of Jay Matternes by Matthew T. Carrano and Kirk R. Johnson, illustrated by Jay Matternes, Smithsonian Books, 2019

ON THE INTERNET

Animal Diversity Web by the University of Michigan Museum of Zoology animaldiversity.org

The Australian Museum australianmuseum.net.au

The International Union for Conservation of Nature (IUCN) Red List • iucnredlist.org

La Brea Tar Pits and Museum • tarpits.org

Natural History Museums of Los Angeles County • nhm.org/educational-resources

Scientific American • scientificamerican.com

The Smithsonian Ocean Portal Educators' Corner ocean.si.edu/educators-corner

Twilight Beasts: Exploring the Magnificent World of Lost Pleistocene Beasts twilightbeasts.org

ABOUT THE AUTHOR AND ILLUSTRATORS

GABRIELLE BALKAN

AUTHOR

Gabrielle Balkan first learned about megafauna on a field trip to the Indiana State Museum in Indianapolis. She loved walking the dark, quiet halls and liked to imagine befriending a woolly mammoth. She now spends her time visiting museums in the Hudson Valley and New York City. She researches and writes on subjects she wants to know more about. When she's not revising, she enjoys reading detective novels, cooking soup, and hiding geocaches for other outdoor enthusiasts to find. Visit her online at gabriellebalkan.com.

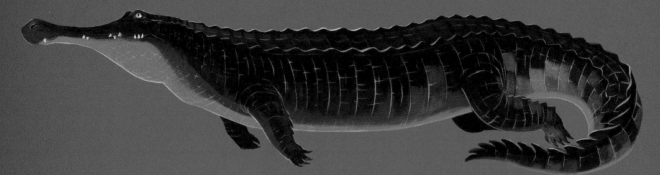

PHUNG NGUYEN QUANG
AND HUYNH KIM LIEN

ILLUSTRATORS

Phung Nguyen Quang and Huynh Kim Lien are Vietnamese illustrators who have collaborated on books published in a number of countries, often under the pen name KAA. Their illustrations are influenced by the folk culture of Vietnam and Asia. Visit them at kaaillustration.com.